HAWAIIAN HERITAGE

Windward face of Nuuanu Pali as it looked in 1795 showing, cen-
ter, past the two men standing on trail, the sheer cliff over which
King Kamehameha's invaders forced Oahu's defenders to death.
*Unknown artist aboard French ship Bonite; Honolulu Academy of
Arts Collection.*

HAWAIIAN HERITAGE

A Brief Illustrated History

by

KATHLEEN DICKENSON MELLEN

HASTINGS HOUSE • PUBLISHERS

New York 22

To HUI KUKA MANAO

with aloha

Contents

[5]

Author's Note

HAWAIIAN HERITAGE is designed to provide quick answers for those interested in Hawaiian history, a colorful and important segment of the Pacific story.

As visitors pour into Hawaii I have noted the questions they ask. The information first sought is: "Who ruled these islands before they became American? When, how, and why were they taken into the Union? What is the history of the Hawaiian people?" I have endeavored to answer these questions through brief biographies of the Hawaiian rulers.

Interest centers next on Hawaii's great houses, such as Iolani Palace (the Capitol), Washington Place (the Governor's Mansion), Queen Emma's home; the famed Mormon temple; Kawaiahao Church; and the Royal Mausoleum, where the flag of Hawaii flies alone over its royal dead. Background descriptions of these and many others are given.

Then there are stories of the great landed estates, such as

that left by Princess Pauahi Bishop for support of The Kamehameha Schools for Hawaiian boys and girls; the Parker ranch (largest privately owned ranch in the world), held by descendants of John Palmer Parker, who came from New England in 1809, married a Hawaiian chiefess and established a family which has played an important role in Hawaiian history.

Niihau, "The Isle of Mystery," which arouses the consuming interest of all newcomers, is described from its beginning to its modern-day pattern. And, since no story of Hawaii would be complete without inclusion of Pele, Goddess of Volcanoes, evidence is given of her continuous rule from the mystical past to the scientific, pragmatic present where she continues to display—at will—her disregard for man-made laws and logical reasoning.

A more intimate picture of the Hawaiians, whom Robert Louis Stevenson called "God's best, His noblest work," may be found in my book IN A HAWAIIAN VALLEY (*Hastings House*) and one of the monarchy over which their ancestors ruled, in my historical tetralogy (*Hastings House*): THE LONELY WARRIOR (Kamehameha the Great); THE MAGNIFICENT MATRIARCH (Queen Kaahumanu); THE GODS DEPART, which completes the story of the Kamehameha Dynasty; and AN ISLAND KINGDOM PASSES, which describes the overthrow of the monarchy and annexation of the Islands to the United States.

HAWAIIAN HERITAGE endeavors to present a kaleidoscopic view of this fascinating island group, now under the flag of the United States, of which Hawaii is the 50th.

K. D. M.

HAWAIIAN HERITAGE

King Kamehameha the Great (1758-1819). *By Louis Choris 1816.*

King Kamehameha the Great
and Queen Kaahumanu

KAMEHAMEHA THE GREAT, "The Lonely Warrior," was born (1758) in the mountains of Kohala, island of Hawaii, whither his mother had fled following an edict by King Alapai that the expected child be slain at birth because of a *kahuna's* prophecy that he would become "a killer of Chiefs and ruler of all the islands."

The baby arrived in the midst of a mighty storm sent by the gods in recognition of the birth of an *alii-nui* (Great One). Lightning split the sky, thunder rent the mountain silence, roaring surf lashed the shore and torrential rains swept the land; and majestically across the midnight sky there sailed a great star plumed with a tail of white fire (Halley's comet, says astronomy).

Fearing discovery of the birthplace by King Alapai's men, loyal retainers hastily carried the baby to a cave high up in the mountains, where, safe from storm and killers, he survived, living to fulfill the prophecy and earn the title Kamehameha the Great.

Kalaniopuu, King of the Island of Hawaii bearing gifts to Captain

Twenty years later Captain James Cook of the British Navy discovered the Hawaiian Islands, which he named the Sandwich Islands for his patron the Earl of Sandwich. Soon afterward young Kamehameha launched a campaign of conquest through which he was to end internecine war between district chiefs and weld the islands into the United Kingdom of Hawaii.

Cook aboard the *Discovery* in Kealakekua Bay. *John Webber 1779*.

By February 1790 he had conquered the islands of Hawaii, Maui and Molokai, and was ready to attack the more heavily populated island of Oahu. From Molokai he sent a messenger to King Kahekili at Waikiki with two stones and the message: "If it is to be war, return the black stone. If peace, the white one."

Keeping both stones, Kahekili told the messenger, "Return to your Chief and tell him that I, an old man, ask that he leave me alone until the black *kapa* covers my body. Then may he come and take this island, after which he can hold sway from here to Tahiti." Uniting the Hawaiian Islands with the motherland of Tahiti had been the dream of many Hawaiian rulers.

So Kamehameha withdrew his forces from Molokai and returned to his home base on the island of Hawaii to wait and prepare for a major campaign. Four years later, when word came of Kahekili's death, he sailed for Oahu in a fleet of a thousand *waakaulua* (double-hulled canoes) and with a formidable fighting force whose native arms were

Home of Kamehameha the Great at Kailua, Kona, Island of Hawaii, seat of government of his United Kingdom of Hawaii.

augmented by two four-pounder swivel-pieces acquired from foreign ships and manned by two Englishmen, Davis and Young.

The fleet landed in pre-dawn darkness on the beach at Kaupo, on windward Oahu between Makapuu and Waimanalo. Then, moving swiftly inland as daybreak lit the land, the magnificently trained invaders met and quickly overwhelmed the unalerted forces of King Kalanikupule (son of King Kahekili). Unable to withstand the conquerors' might, the defenders retreated up Nuuanu Valley. The battle ended on the brink of Nuuanu Pali (precipice), where the remnant of Kalanikupule's army was forced over

Here he held Court until his death in 1819. *Paul Emmert 1816.* (Upon the site now stands the luxurious King Kamehameha Hotel.)

the rim to death in the rubble at the base of the sheer cliff.

Proving himself as wise in peace as he had been mighty in war, Kamehameha, after persuading the island of Kauai to join the union voluntarily, set about to strengthen his United Kingdom and to enrich the lives of his people. So successful was he that within a few years British Captain Beechy wrote: *History will rank him, however limited his sphere, among the great men of his time.*

Said Russian Navy Commander von Kotzebue: "He is a man of great wisdom. Giving his people only things he considers useful, he tries to increase the *happiness*, not the *wants*, of his people." Commented another visitor: "Justice is the premise that pervades his life and thinking."

Hawaiians said, lovingly, "He is our Father. He is the *taro* of the land, the giver of life and source of all our happiness."

Waipio Valley, Island of Hawaii, Kohala District, where Kamehameha the Great was hidden away for the first five years of his life. Artist unknown; Honolulu Academy of Arts.

Queen Kaahumanu (1772-1832). *By Louis Choris 1816.*

According to custom, Kamehameha had many wives. Most important of them were the aristocratic Keopuolani, mother of the heirs apparent, known as "The Sacred Wife," and barren Kaahumanu, who was called "The Favorite Wife." Majestic physically and brilliant mentally, Kaahumanu was his constant companion and the only wife who met and talked with visiting foreigners. Captain Vancouver of the British Admiralty described her as "the most beautiful woman in the South Seas."

While the Sacred Wife lived hedged about by strict formalities, Kaahumanu confidently rode the sweeping tides of a new era. Working vigorously for the solution of problems growing out of the swiftly changing times, she was guided always by the passionate love for Kamehameha which formed a shining thread in the fabric of her life.

He said of her: "She is as beautiful as a *lehua* blossom. She rides the waves like a bird; she knows the heartbeat of the people. There is none like her in all the land."

[17]

Royal Temple at Kealakekua, viewed from the Bay, where Kamehameha worshiped as a young chief and as monarch of the United Kingdom when his Court was at near-by Kailua. *Louis Choris 1816.*

On May 8, 1819, in the glow of fame, glory and great achievement, Kamehameha died in his grass palace beside the sea at Kailua, Kona, island of Hawaii. To those present he said, "Tell my people I have planted in the soil of our land the roots of a plan for their happiness. It is necessary only that they cultivate the ground that there may be growth and development of the plan, for it is inexhaustible. . . ." Then his voice faded, and was stilled.

While the land echoed with bitter wailing, trusted retainers carried the bones of the beloved hero to a secret sepulcher somewhere in the cliffs of the Kona coast. Its exact location remains unknown today and Hawaiians rejoice that "Only the stars know the resting place of Kamehameha."

To insure the continuation of his policies, Kamehameha had created the office of *kuhina-nui* (Prime Minister) for Kaahumanu, stipulating that she be co-ruler with his son Liholiho, who was to reign as Kamehameha II.

[18]

However, the vital, imperious, strong-willed Kaahumanu, known to history as the Magnificent Matriarch, quickly became the real ruler of the kingdom. "She reproduced Kamehameha's character reflected in her womanhood," wrote historian Manley Hopkins; "it was the moon 'taking up the wondrous tale' after the setting of her lord from whom she derived her light."

After a full and vigorous life Kaahumanu died in 1832. Her going was recorded in the Court *mele*:

> "She has gone from us to the Court of Kane,
> Treading royally the red-streaked path of rosy dawn
> As her spirit glides away to the far regions
> Beyond Kahiki.
>
> Oh our Beloved One! Our departed one!
> We are torn with passionate grief.
> Without you there is nothing
> We flee together!"

Royal hula dancers at the Court of Kamehameha the Great at Kailua, Kona, costumed in fine tapa, the skirt of the leader distinguished by the knot in front (grass skirt is a recent importation from South Sea islands). Louis Choris 1816.

King Kamehameha II (1797-1824). *By Sir John Hayter, London,*
1824.

King Kamehameha II and Queen Kamamalu

FIRST-BORN OF KAMEHAMEHA the Great and his Sacred Wife
Keopuolani was a son whom they called Kalaninui Liholiho
(The Heavens with Great Glowing). The childhood of this
cherished heir apparent was guided entirely by his delicately
bred mother, whose gentle nature he had inherited. As he
grew older Court priests trained him in religious duties,
which he liked, and in affairs of state, which interested him
less and of which he gained no practical knowledge. Succeeding to the throne of the kingdom at age twenty-two, he
was ill-equipped by temperament or training to handle complex problems arising from a sudden influx of foreigners.

Able, ambitious co-ruler Dowager Queen Kaahumanu,
taking advantage of the situation, quickly increased her own
powers and soon became the actual ruler of the kingdom.
Confused and frustrated, Liholiho decided to visit England
for consultation with King George. Accompanied by his
Favorite Wife, the lovely Kamamalu, and a retinue, Liholiho
sailed for England, arriving in May, 1824.

[21]

Immediately the royal party was placed in charge of the Honorable Fredrick Bynge, who lodged them in fashionable Clarendon Hotel. After handsome Windsor uniforms had been provided for the king and the latest Parisian gowns for the queen, they were presented to London society and became "the rage of the day." The press described the king as "royal in every sense of the word" and his queen consort as "warm from nature's heart." Their portraits were painted by Sir John Hayter.

A conference with King George was arranged but before the meeting date tragedy struck with shocking suddenness. Queen Kamamalu became ill with measles, against which Hawaiians had no immunity, and died quickly. Grief-stricken, King Liholiho followed her in death within a week, despite all efforts of the Court physician.

Stunned, the people of London hastened to express their sympathy while members of the royal entourage poured

The residential complex (several grass houses, each for a specific purpose, was the customary home) occupied by Lord Byron, commander of *HBMS Blonde,* when he visited Hilo after delivering the bodies of King Kamehameha II and Consort Kamamalu at Honolulu in May, 1825. His ship rides at anchor in the estuary then at mouth of the Wailuku River. *Robert Dampier 1825.*

Queen Kamamalu (1802-1824). *By Sir John Hayter, London, 1824.*

out their grief in a wailing *kanikau* (bereavement chant). Following official rites in St. Martin's Church, the handsome bronze caskets were borne aboard *HBMS Blonde*, in command of the Right Honorable (George Anson) Lord Byron, cousin of the poet, the ship sailing for Hawaii in September, 1824. Word of the deaths had reached Honolulu before arrival of the *Blonde* in May, 1825, and the shore was lined with thousands of people as the ship came into Honolulu Harbor.

The funeral cortege, led by fifty Hawaiians carrying towering feather *kahilis* and followed by marines from the *Blonde*, moved slowly along a reed-carpeted street lined with wailing subjects to Iolani Palace, where the royal dead were to lie in state. Remembered sorrowfully by the people was the young queen's prophetic farewell on their departure for England:

"Farewell my beloved people. Ye skies, ye plains, ye mountains and sea—farewell to thee. Alas, alas! Farewell to thee!"

[23]

King Kamehameha III (1813-1854). By contemporary painter, signature illegible, in Iolani Palace Throne Room.

King Kamehameha III and Queen Kalama

ANOTHER SON of Kamehameha the Great and Keopuolani, born 1813, was named Kauike-aouli (Surrounded by Black Clouds) by the Court prophet, who said, "Foreigners will always surround him. They are the black clouds. He cannot escape his destiny."

At the age of eight he entered the Chiefs' Children's School, conducted by the American missionaries, Mr. and Mrs. Amos Cooke, where he was given a good education. At twelve, following the death of his elder brother Liholiho in London, he was proclaimed King Kamehameha III. Dowager Queen Kaahumanu served as Regent during his minority and he came into full control only after her death in 1832. He married Kalama, daughter of a lesser chief. They had no children.

The reign of Kamehameha III covered thirty-one eventful, danger-fraught years, during which his kingdom was constantly harassed by the great world powers that sought control of his beautiful little islands. Threatened first with loss of sovereignty by France, they were later seized and

OLDEST-FRAME BUILDING
IN THESE ISLANDS
Occupied, October 1821.
VISITORS WELCOME

Incongruously stark in the grass-thatched Honolulu of 1821, this house was a breath of home-sweet-home to the New England missionaries lucky enough to rate residence therein. Pre-fabricated, it was shipped knocked down around Cape Horn and set up in the Missionary Compound, where it stands today in good condition. *Hawaiian Archives.*

held briefly by a British naval officer but were returned at the command of Queen Victoria. American residents endeavored to bring about their annexation to the United States.

Alarmed by these continuing pressures, the young monarch called a meeting of the High Chiefs, who warned: "The big fish are coming up from the bottom of the ocean and will try to eat up the little fish. Therefore get your servants ready for the time of need." Among themselves they said, "Our little king is gentle, trusting and has a woman's heart. He cannot fight these foreigners alone. We must stand close by him."

Queen Kalama (1817-1870). *Hawaiian Archives*.

Some resident aliens urged appointment of themselves as advisers "because we know best how to deal with other foreigners" and the king, feeling it wise to do so, met protests of his subjects by saying, "Trust me, oh my people. I do this that we may live in peace. You are first in my heart; it is for your safety that I pray when I weep alone in the blackness of night." But the people were still fearful, some believing that they were being punished for accepting the foreign religion; "And now our own gods have gone away," they wailed.

The foreign advisers began immediately to change the kingdom's form of government, revising it until there remained scarcely a vestige of that established by Kamehameha the Great. Heart and center of these changes was the Great *Mahele*—a division of the lands of the kingdom traditionally held in trust for the people by their rulers. This one piece of legislation was to destroy forever the ancient pattern of Hawaiian life.

Under the *Mahele*, one-third of the land was to be retained by the Crown, one-third divided among the chiefs, one-third to the commoners. For the first time, land could be bought and sold. Having no knowledge of private ownership of land, the commoners and many chiefs soon found themselves landless. Wrote Hawaiian historian Samuel Kamakau:

"Ownership of the land by the king was the rock that formed the anchor of our safety. Now the rock has been shattered by the storm."

Grief-stricken by belated realization of the danger to his people, the Little King who had loved them so deeply and tenderly died December 15, 1854. He was only forty-one.

Kamakau reported: "The sound of wailing rose from all parts of the land as the people raised their voices in lamentations to heaven that Ka-ne might hear and pour down rains to fall as tears upon the earth."

King Kamehameha IV and Queen Emma

PRINCE ALEXANDER LIHOLIHO, twenty-year-old grandson of Kamehameha the Great and an adopted son of Kamehameha III, was proclaimed King Kamehameha IV December 15, 1854. The people proudly called him "Our aristocratic king." Tall, slender, erect, he wore a British Windsor uniform on all official occasions and modeled his Court after that of Queen Victoria, who entertained him in 1850 while he was touring Europe with American missionary Gerrit P. Judd, M.D.

Intellectually brilliant, Alexander had a deeply sensitive nature and a strongly dedicated soul. The ills of his nation, his people, burned hotly in his heart and he entered upon his reign with firm resolve to preserve his kingdom from foreign intrigue and to restore the health of his people, rapidly being decimated by alien disease. To these goals he devoted the full pattern of his life.

In 1856 he married Emma Kalani-kau-maka Rooke, adopted daughter of Britisher Thomas Rooke, M.D. She

King Kamehameha IV (1834-1863). *Hawaiian Archives.*

was a grand-niece of Kamehameha the Great and grand-daughter of Englishman John Young. The Court they established was elegant, gracious and British in manner. Invitations to their soirees were eagerly sought by the foreign colony.

Always uppermost in the minds of the young rulers, however, was the welfare of their people. At their request the Anglican Church of England was established in the Islands, with pastoral schools for Hawaiian boys and girls. Their crowning achievement was the Queen's Hospital, primarily for "indigent Hawaiians" but open to other races when space permitted. It was described by the press as "A memorial of the love of the King and Queen for the Hawaiian race."

Queen Emma (1836-1885). *Hawaiian Archives.*

On May 20, 1858, amid great national rejoicing, a royal heir was born: Albert Edward Kauike-aouli Lei-o-papa o Kamehameha. The first two names were those of his godfather, the Prince of Wales, who with his royal mother Queen Victoria sponsored the christening, Her Majesty sending a costly silver cup and marble baptismal font.

Tragically, the royal heir who had entered the world with such loving fanfare died at the age of four. It was a blow from which his father never recovered. One year later, in November, 1863, the proud young king who had begun his reign with such high hopes died quietly in his sleep, at his side the devoted consort whose valorous spirit had delighted him in days of happiness and sustained him in hours of sorrow.

[31]

Queen Emma survived her husband by twenty-two years—years filled with devoted service to her people, travel in Europe, where she became a close friend of Queen Victoria, and finally a peaceful end in Hawaii, enshrined in the hearts of her people as "the most beloved *alii* in all the land."

Said the newspapers: "She shed luster upon her race." Hawaiians cried bitterly, "*Ua ohi paka-aki ia aku nui a ko po*" ("The night is taking them one by one.")

Prince of Hawaii (1858-1862). *Hawaiian Archives.*

The Bachelor Kings,
Kamehameha V and Lunalilo

PRINCE LOT KAMEHAMEHA, thirty-three-year-old brother of
Kamehameha IV, was proclaimed King of Hawaii on November 30, 1863, as Kamehameha V. Of stern visage and
reserved personality, he was called by foreigners "the last
of the olden chiefs." Hawaiians referred to him by his
"sacred" name, Kapu-a-iwa—archaic Hawaiian connoting
"The inner being is mysterious and incomprehensible." And
so he was to foreigners and natives alike: cold, aloof, and
wholly lacking in his late brother's love of splendor.

Never close in spirit to his people, Kamehameha V
nonetheless fought constantly to protect them against the
power-hungry foreigners whose demands he resisted strongly
and successfully. Embittered by the loss of his childhood
sweetheart, the beautiful Princess Pauahi, who had married
the American Charles R. Bishop, he took an oath of celibacy
and, although he later developed a sincere admiration for
Mr. Bishop, he never married.

The king's first official act was revision of the Constitu-

[33]

King Kamehameha V (1830-1872). *Hawaiian Archives.*

tion to limit the franchise and to increase power of the throne. To protests of the foreign colony he replied coldly, "The present Constitution was drawn up by the foreigners for their own benefit. I do not approve of that Constitution and threats against me are rubbish." Without further argument he proclaimed a new Constitution drawn up by himself, his Cabinet and members of the Supreme Court.

Next, despite his personal dislike for the alien civilization crowding in upon his land, he set about to prepare his kingdom for its apparently inescapable destiny as commercial center of the Pacific. An extensive program of public works included a new government building, the Alii-o-lani, a Royal Barracks, post office, customs house, school buildings and the widening and deepening of Honolulu Harbor.

Greatest problems were, first, the sugar planters' demand for a reciprocity treaty with the United States to admit their product duty-free; and, second, the increased importation of laborers for the plantations.

The latter was bitterly fought by Hawaiians who warned, "Some day these people they are bringing in will take over our beautiful land and we, the children of the soil, will no longer control the home of our ancestors." To this the king replied firmly, "We are fighting a relentless battle for survival. I am doing the best I can to save us. Trust me, oh my people."

Caught in this crossfire of opposing pressures, the king battled valiantly for preservation of his kingdom until finally even his robust health cracked under the strain. His physician's diagnosis was "kidney trouble with dropsical complications." Hawaiians came in great numbers to pray for this strange, cold man with whom they felt no close rapport but for whom they had great admiration.

As death neared, the king begged his beloved Pauahi to become his successor but she, happily married, declined. He then decided to leave the question of succession to the Legislature, as permitted by the Constitution.

On the morning of December 11, 1872, in the ninth year of his reign and with the city garlanded in honor of his forty-second birthday, the cold, stern but deeply patriotic king died. His death marked the end of the Kamehameha Dynasty, and also the end of an era of Hawaiian history.

King Lunalilo (1835-1874). *Hawaiian Archives.*

King Lunalilo

Prince William Lunalilo, grand-nephew of Kamehameha the Great, was a versatile young man of many talents. Musical, witty, pleasure-loving and gay, his quick mind and charming personality endeared him to nobility and commoners alike. Particularly did the commoners adore him and he returned their love in full measure.

So, despite his irresponsible approach to life, his total disinterest in affairs of state and a decided weakness for strong drink, the people unanimously elected him ruler of the kingdom to succeed the stern but able Kamehameha V. A gay philanderer who followed the light of love where he found it, Lunalilo at age thirty-eight was still unmarried.

His kingship was short and tragic. Confused by cares of state and upset by pressures of the foreigners, he turned to drink and his always delicate body succumbed to an incipient lung disease. After a brief reign of one year and twenty-five days, death came to him on February 3, 1874. Having been unaware of the seriousness of his illness, the people were stunned. Newspapers reported: "There was not a sound, a wail. Only a dead silence."

To "the poor, destitute and infirm people of Hawaiian blood" the King left his large landed estate, with instructions that home and support be provided for them. He requested that he be buried not in the Royal Mausoleum but among the commoners in the grounds of Kawaiahao Church. Prior to the completion of a proper tomb for him, the body was interred at the Royal Mausoleum with full royal honors, including the customary twenty-one-gun salute.

A year later, when the casket was transferred to Kawaiahao, requests from the King's devoted followers that formal ceremonies be repeated were carried out, excepting only the formal salute. Not from legend nor imaginative hearsay but from contemporary newspapers comes this report:

"As the royal casket was being lowered into the tomb there swept across the clear blue sky a flash of lightning followed by resounding claps of thunder—21 of them—to provide proper royal salute."

Thus, in death, the gods of old gave rightful recognition to King William Lunalilo, the gay, lovable ruler known to history as "The People's King."

King Kalakaua and Queen Kapiolani

HIGH CHIEF DAVID KALAKAUA, by vote of the Legislature, became King of Hawaii on February 12, 1874, at the age of thirty-eight. He was founder of a new royal dynasty. Descended from a noble line of chiefs, he further strengthened his right to rulership by marriage to the High Chiefess Kapiolani of the royal line from the island of Kauai.

Backed by the sugar planters in exchange for a pledge to work for a reciprocity treaty with the United States, the new king was supported also by the foreign diplomats, among whom he was exceedingly popular. They described him as "suave, scholarly, a gentleman of fine education, polished manners and good breeding."

Hawaiians loved him for his pledge that the "watchword" of his reign would be Ho'ouli Lahui (Increase of the People). "If our land is filled with babies," he said, "we can be strong and independent." Equally interested in the welfare of the people, Queen Consort Kapiolani later willed her fortune to found and maintain a maternity home, "that

King Kalakaua (1836-1891). *Hawaiian Archives.*

our babies may live." Childless himself, the King appointed
his younger brother Leleihoku heir apparent, and his sister,
Liliuokalani, second in succession.

King Kalakaua's reign was filled with drama and great
events, its pattern one of brilliant sunshine alternating with
dark shadows as he endeavored to bring happiness to the
lives of his people and at the same time satisfy those foreigners who were interested only in financial gain. Confirm-
ing his pledge to the sugar planters, he went to Washington
and negotiated a reciprocity treaty which allowed Hawaiian

Queen Kapiolani (1834-1899). *Hawaiian Archives.*

sugar to enter the United States duty-free.

Unfortunately for his country, however, the swift increase of wealth resulting from the treaty spawned many difficulties, chief of which was an ever increasing demand for more labor. To offset this augmented alien influence, Kalakaua inaugurated a renaissance of Hawaiian culture through revival of ancient dances, sports, music and chants, recording the history of his people back into the mists of time. Most important of these chants was the *Kumulipo* (The Chant of Creation) which tells the story of Polynesia

[41]

for countless centuries. Formerly transmitted orally, the important chant was now, for the first time, recorded for posterity.

This rich revival of Hawaiian culture attracted world attention. From East and West came musicians, writers, gay *bon vivants*, and soon the Court of King Kalakaua became known throughout the world as "The Court of the Bohemians."

Desire for increased knowledge prompted His Majesty to make a trip around the world. He was warmly received at all the courts of Asia and Europe and on his return filled his newly built Iolani Palace with treasures collected as gifts and by purchase.

On February 12, 1883, King Kalakaua and his Queen were crowned in formal ceremony. Three years later he sent a commission to negotiate an alliance with his fellow Polynesians of the Samoan Kingdom. The foreigners in Hawaii, fearing curtailment of their own powers, immediately launched newspaper attacks upon him (today copied by many writers as factual history) of such intensity as to prompt revolts and counter-revolts which kept the kingdom in constant turmoil for several years.

In November, 1890, King Kalakaua, his health seriously impaired, sought medical care in San Francisco. There he died, January 20, 1891. Thus ended a brilliant era of Hawaiian history under a ruler known and loved around the world as "The Merrie Monarch of the Pacific."

Queen Liliuokalani

PRINCESS LILIUOKALANI, fifty-three-year-old sister of King Kalakaua, was proclaimed Queen of Hawaii January 29, 1891. Her brief reign, fraught with turmoil and heartaches, ended in January, 1893, with the overthrow of the Monarchy. Between those two dates were many tragic events.

In August, 1862, the Princess had married American John Owen Dominis and both had been active in court life and in government for thirty years. His death, seven months after she came to the throne, was the first of many tragedies to mar her life in years to come.

Of brilliant mind and strong character, the Queen entered upon her duties with firm determination to regain control of the government wrested from the people in 1887 by a "reform" Constitution forced upon King Kalakaua by foreign commercial interests. Her attempt to replace it with one restricting the vote to native Hawaiians and those foreigners who had become citizens of the kingdom was used as an excuse for her overthrow.

Queen Liliuokalani (1839-1917). *Hawaiian Archives.*

Prince Consort John
(1851-1887).
Hawaiian Archives.

The insurrection was bloodless, the Queen advising her people not to fight but to await America's action on a petition sent by the usurpers to President Grover Cleveland asking for annexation of the Islands to the United States. Cleveland rejected the request, saying, "To take the Islands from the native people would be inconsistent with American honor, integrity and morality." The usurpers then set up "The Republic of Hawaii."

Encouraged by Cleveland's attitude and also by thousands of letters of sympathy from the American people, Hawaiians waited, confident that the United States would restore their Queen. But after two years when no help was forthcoming, they staged a counter-revolt in January, 1895. It failed. Queen Liliuokalani, several hundred Hawaiians and a few white sympathizers were tried for "treason."

The Queen was sentenced to twenty-five years at hard

labor (never carried out). Death sentences were given leaders of the revolt, life imprisonment to others. Angry warnings from Washington, however, forced release of all within a year.

While a prisoner in one room of Iolani Palace, where she had ruled as queen, Liliuokalani composed two beautiful songs which live today in world affection: *Aloha Oe* and *The Queen's Prayer*. After her release she went to Washington, where she received great ovations and was showered with gifts and loving attention by the American people. A newsman described her as "a woman of singular grace which is majesty itself."

But unfortunately for the Hawaiians their cause had become entangled with an American crisis. The Spanish-American war, exploding suddenly, made Hawaii's strategic position in the Pacific of utmost importance for America's protection, so, despite a genuine sympathy for the Hawaiians and over the protests of many members of Congress, the United States annexed the Islands.

On August 12, 1898, while the Hawaiians wept quietly in their homes, the Hawaiian flag came down and the Stars and Stripes went up over Iolani Palace.

America's first move was to restore the franchise to native Hawaiians, who in the next election came once again into control of their homeland. Other acts of justice and kindness won their hearts and today Hawaiians are among America's most loyal and devoted citizens.

Queen Liliuokalani devoted the rest of her life to working for the welfare of her people. Her large estate was left for the care and protection of Hawaiian orphans. Not long before her death in 1917 she raised—for the first time—the American flag over her home, Washington Place, as token of her allegiance to the United States.

Princess Likelike and Princess Kaiulani

PRINCESS LIKELIKE, born in 1851, was a younger sister of Queen Liliuokalani. She married Britisher Archibald Cleghorn and their one child, daughter Kaiulani (born in 1875), was designated by the Queen as heir apparent.

Gay and impulsive by nature, Princess Likelike was adored by her people and was also a favorite of foreign diplomats, who called her "the most gracious flowering of the Hawaiian race." Beautiful and vivacious, she was equally poised as Governor of the island of Hawaii or as hostess of Ainahau, the Waikiki Cleghorn mansion set in a large botanical garden created by her husband, a noted amateur naturalist.

But tragically, as with many members of Hawaiian nobility in post-discovery Hawaii, Likelike's life-span was short. She died at thirty, leaving motherless the twelve-year-old Princess Kaiulani, whose father prepared to send her, the heir apparent, to London for special training in her royal duties. Before her departure, famed author Robert Louis

Princess Likelike (1851-1887). *Hawaiian Archives.*

Stevenson came to Hawaii and the two became devoted friends. As they sat together under a big banyan tree in the Cleghorn grounds, he told the shy little Princess many tales of his homeland, soon to welcome her, and wrote a poem beginning:

"From her land to mine she goes/ The island maiden, the island rose/ Light of heart and bright of face/ This daughter of a double race."

Kaiulani left for England in May, 1889. Four years

Princess Kaiulani (1875-1899). *Baker Archives.*

later, after the overthrow of the monarchy she was being trained to rule, she went to Washington in response to her peoples' request that she "present our plea for justice." There she enchanted all with whom she came in contact. Newspapers described her as a "delicate, exquisite beauty . . . a finished musician, an artist, a linguist." Her manners, they said, "are those of the born aristocrat."

In a proclamation to the American people she said in part: "If you are the noble-minded people I believe you to be you will not permit this outrage . . ." Their response to her plea was a deluge of letters to Congress denouncing "this robbery of her birthright." But the tide of history was moving swiftly, with the Hawaiian Islands caught in a current of world events stirred up by the Spanish-American war. Restoration of the throne she sought proved impossible.

In 1897, one year before annexation of the Islands to the United States, the gentle, gallant little Princess returned to her homeland. But she was not long to survive the kingdom she had sought to save. Always delicate in health, she appeared, said her friends, "to be slowly fading away."

Seven months after the American flag was raised officially over Iolani Palace, at dawn of March 6, 1899, while Hawaiian skies wept copiously and her people wailed their bitter grief, Kaiulani's gentle spirit joined those of her royal ancestors. Wrote a newsman:

"Like a white dove, Kaiulani's spirit has flown to the Elysian fields of immortality, but memory of her virtues will linger like the fragrance of the flowers she loved so well."

Prince David and Princess Abigail Kawananakoa

PRINCE DAVID KAWANANAKOA, nephew of King Kalakaua's Consort Kapiolani, was designated heir to the Hawaiian throne, succeeding Princess Kaiulani, to whom he was betrothed. Following her death, he married (in 1902) Abigail Wahihi-ka-ahuula Campbell, daughter of a Hawaiian mother and a Scotch-Irish father, James A. Campbell. They had three children: David Kalakaua, who died without issue; and daughters Kapiolani, who had one son and two daughters; and Liliuokalani, who had one daughter.

Prince David was educated in England, where he was described as "dignified, reserved, with gentlemanly manner and bearing." Hawaiians said of him, admiringly, "He lives his rank." This proud prince of Hawaii died of a heart attack in 1908 at the age of forty.

Princess Abigail, his strikingly beautiful twenty-six-year-old widow, soon took up her travels again, returning to European capitals where she had reigned as a belle before her marriage. In 1924 she came back to live permanently in

Princess Abigail Kawananakoa (1882-1945). *Courtesy Kapiolani Kawananakoa.*

her Islands, where she quickly became a "power-behind-the-throne" in Territorial Hawaii. Famed for her political skill, sparkling wit, majestic beauty and the brilliance of her entertaining, she was described by author Armien von Tempsky:

"She would be a Princess in any language, any age; Cleopatra, Circe and Aspasia all rolled into one. Six feet tall but as delicately boned as a gazelle . . . richness envelopes her as if she had been born at high noon in golden sunlight. People standing near her look as if their blood had been diluted with water."

Prince David Kawananakoa (1868-1908). *Courtesy Kapiolani Kawananakoa.*

Invitations to her home were eagerly sought by the great and near-great from all parts of the world. Visiting royalty from Europe and Asia deferred to her wishes before accepting invitations even from official Hawaii. On formal occasions she was the Princess Royale; informally, a witty, sophisticated, delightful companion, her brilliant mind a joy to her friends and cause of dismay for those who feared her great influence among high officials in Washington. Strong-willed like other famed Polynesian matriarchs, the fabric of her soul was firmly woven.

Granddaughters of Prince and Princess Kawananakoa: Poomaikalani (left) *Billy Howell*; Kapiolani, the Marchesa Filipo Marignoli (right) of Rome. *Chergo, Rome;*

Kekaulike (below) leading a Kamehameha Day parade. *Honolulu Advertiser.*

"The Incomparable Kamokila" Campbell, sister of Princess Kawananakoa. Artist, musician, politician, ardent Royalist, Keeper of Hawaiian lore and tradition, hostess extraordinaire. *Honolulu Advertiser.*

On April 12, 1945, death came suddenly to this distinguished Hawaiian Princess and as her bold, courageous spirit took flight a terrific storm swept the valley near her home, torrential rain, thunder and lightning rending the sky as in days of old when the gods joined Hawaiians in joy at the birth or grief at the passing of a great *Alii.*

Again, as her casket was borne down the stairway of the Kalakaua crypt in the Royal Mausoleum to be placed beside that of her husband, Prince David, there came a brief heavy downpour. Then the clouds parted to reveal in all its splendor the great mountain Lanihuli, which forms a backdrop for the Mausoleum, its peak crowned with a perfect rainbow.

Reported the Honolulu *Advertiser:* "Hawaii's last tie with the pomp and circumstance of its scintillating monarchial era was severed yesterday as Hawaiian skies wept for their *alii.* . . . She was a gracious, womanly Princess, bestowing with lavish hand upon the needy of her people, counseling them in ways of righteous living . . . a master of statecraft, her influence extended to the seat of government in Washington. . . . Her memory is enshrined in our hearts, her spirit remains beside her people undying."

The Kamehameha Schools
and Bishop Museum

PRINCESS BERNICE PAUAHI BISHOP, great-granddaughter of
Kamehameha I and heir to the vast Kamehameha lands,
could have ruled as Queen of Hawaii but preferred instead
the life of a private citizen as wife of her American husband,
Charles Reed Bishop, with whom she worked for the guid-
ance and strengthening of the young people of her race.
Her landed inheritance was willed to endow schools for
Hawaiian boys and girls.

Today The Kamehameha Schools, on a 600-acre hillside overlooking Honolulu, hold the hopes and dreams of
the Hawaiian race, the key to its survival. Encompassing
more than a mere formal education, their aim, according to
former president Harold Kent, "has been to provide Hawaiians with a strong academic basis for competing with other
races yet at the same time leave unchanged their own
basically fine qualities."

With a 1963 enrollment of more than 2000, there are
plans for increasing the number as rapidly as facilities can

Princess Pauahi Bishop (1831-1884). *Hawaiian Archives.*

be added. Training goes from kindergarten through high school, with courses ranging from the practical to the esthetic. About seventy per cent of the graduates go on to college each year.

For girls, in addition to academic courses, there are three practice cottages for training in home management, including care of babies loaned by Hawaiian mothers. For boys, studies range from technical to academic. Among the many departments are a radio station, a wood-carving shop, motor pool, an agricultural project and linotype and book-binding operations where they publish a newspaper and books for sale. Also, Kamehameha is a grade-A military school.

Garlanding the whole scholastic program is Hawaiian music, stressed from kindergarten to graduation. Recordings of The Kamehameha Schools choir are sold and loved around the world.

Thus the spirit of a Hawaiian Princess who died in 1884 continues to live through the young people of her race who visit the Royal Mausoleum each year on her birthday and pay tribute to their royal benefactress with flowers, song and prayers of gratitude. In today's strife-torn world this great institution stands like a gleaming light of hope.

"We who work with the boys and girls of Kamehameha have a great moral obligation," says President James W.

Kamehameha Schools co-eds training for motherhood in Practice Cottage with babies loaned by patrons. *The Kamehameha Schools.*

Kamehameha Schools cadet and co-ed secretary. *The Kamehameha Schools.*

Bushong. "We must succeed, as a tribute to the memory of the wise and gracious Princess whose foresight made possible the bright day now dawning for the native children of Hawaii. We expect The Kamehameha Schools to provide the state of Hawaii and the nation with outstanding citizens and leaders. We are confident. Truly the greatest triumphs of the Hawaiian people lie before them."

The Bishop Museum

Charles Reed Bishop, husband of the philanthropic Princess, established (1889) in her memory the Bernice Pauahi Bishop Museum. Today, under the able direction of Dr. Roland W. Force, it is considered the scientific center of the Pacific and pursues a wide range of research. There,

Panorama of The Kamehameha Schools. *The Kamehameha Schools.*

visitors may see a varied and fascinating collection of Hawaiiana and objects from other Pacific islands, a fine modern Planetarium-Observatory and a Hall of Pacific Life, presenting salient features of the geography and biology of the vast Pacific area.

Kamehameha students, working at the Museum as part of their scholastic training, gain there a broader knowledge and understanding of their racial heritage. Visitors to the Islands, welcomed at both Museum and Schools, find in these institutions many of the answers they seek concerning the Hawaiian story.

The Royal Mausoleum

First departure from the ancient Hawaiian custom of secret burial of the nobility was a crypt in the ground of Iolani Palace, a site now marked by a grassy mound within a low iron fence. Then, in 1863, Kamehameha IV set aside a plot in Nuuanu Valley for a Royal Mausoleum. Its first unit, a small Gothic chapel, served as temporary crypt until 1884, when a separate one was built for members of the Kamehameha Dynasty, followed by another for the Kalakaua Dynasty. Today the Royal Mausoleum is the only place in all Hawaii where the Hawaiian flag flies alone—a privilege granted by the United States at the time of annexation.

Entrance to the grounds is by heavy wrought-iron gates bearing the seal of the Kingdom of Hawaii. Circling the grounds is a driveway lined with royal palms whose gleaming white trunks, topped with clustered fronds, stand like royal *kahilis* on guard in the sacred grounds dotted with shrubs and flowering trees.

Students of The Kamehameha Schools at The Royal Mausoleum paying homage to the memory of Princess Pauahi. *The Kamehameha Schools.*

The Kamehameha crypt was completed in 1887 and on September 9 received the Kamehamehas, from Kamehameha II to Princess Pauahi, borne in midnight silence by the light of *kukui* torches from the Gothic chapel to their last resting place, now marked by a brown marble cenotaph and two *tabu* sticks, traditional emblems of Royalty's presence.

Five foreigners who had married royalty also rest in the Royal Mausoleum. Near the Kamehameha crypt are the tombs of American Charles R. Bishop, husband of Princess Pauahi, and Britisher Thomas Rooke, foster father of Queen Emma. Behind the Gothic chapel is the tomb of John Young, English adviser to Kamehameha I and grandfather of Queen Emma. Also entombed in the sacred ground is Britisher Robert C. Wyllie, who served as loyal Minister of Foreign Affairs for the Kingdom under three rulers.

[63]

A crypt for the Kalakaua Dynasty was completed in 1910. A stairway, before which stand two gold-tipped *tabu* sticks, leads down to a marble vault in the form of a Greek cross. At the head of the vault rest King Kalakaua and Queen Consort Kapiolani; along the sides, other members of the Kalakaua line, each space marked with a gold-lettered name plate. Two foreigners are included in this crypt: American John Owen Dominis, Prince Consort of Queen Liliuokalani, and Britisher Archibald Cleghorn, husband of Princess Likelike.

Those who witnessed the ceremonies transferring members of the Kalakaua Dynasty from chapel to vault noted a special tenderness in the voice of singers as the casket of the greatly beloved young Princess Kaiulani was lowered into the tomb. Last transferred, with proud, dramatic ceremonies, was that of King Kalakaua.

Seven years later, in 1917, another casket was carried down the stairway to the accompaniment of bitter tears and wailing: that of the last ruler, Queen Liliuokalani. *Aloha Oe*, her own beautiful composition, was sung by voices that trembled with emotion while "tears fell like drops of blood from the hearts of her people."

Three more spaces were yet to be filled. In January, 1922, Prince Kuhio Kalanianaole, who had served as Hawaii's Delegate to Congress for twenty years, was entombed. In April, 1945, followed Princess Kawananakoa. With interment of her son, David, in 1954, the crypt was sealed forever.

Only Kamehameha the Great is missing. His bones are hidden in a secret cave on the Kona coast, concealed forever, it is hoped, from the prying world that now roams his islands at will. "The Lonely One" in life, he remains the lonely one in death. Such would have been his wish.

Washington Place

WASHINGTON PLACE, once the home of Queen Liliuokalani, is now the official residence of Hawaii's Governors. For more than one hundred years it has been the center of historic events. Its walls have echoed both joy and sorrow and the story of its beginnings is as dramatic as its subsequent history.

Clipper-ship captain John Dominis, Boston-born Italian, after many perilous voyages around the horn in the China trade decided to make Hawaii his home. Arriving with his wife and nine-year-old son John in 1837, he settled down and in 1842 started building an American colonial-type home to be the realization of his dreams.

The stately pillared mansion was completed in 1847 and Captain Dominis, to seek furnishings worthy of its grace and dignity, sailed once more for China. The brig *William Neilson*, in which he sailed, was never heard of again.

Mrs. Dominis and her son John continued to live in

Washington Place, former home of Queen Liliuokalani, now the
Governor's Mansion. *Hawaii Visitors Bureau.*

the great mansion but rented a portion of it to the United States Legation, headed by Commissioner Anthony Ten-Eyke, who with her permission raised the American flag in the grounds on February 22, 1848, and formally notified King Kamehameha III that "On this day . . . the beautiful and universally admired mansion of Mrs. Dominis has been christened Washington Place in honor of George Washington."

Fourteen years later, September 10, 1862, young John Dominis brought home to Washington Place his bride, the High Chiefess Lydia Kamakaeha. She was the sister of High Chief David Kalakaua, who, on becoming king in 1874, named her heir apparent under the title of Princess Liliuokalani.

In 1891 Liliuokalani succeeded to the throne and reigned for two tumultuous years. Unsuccessful in her attempt to rescue her kingdom from foreign domination, she was overthrown in 1893. Until her death in 1917 Washington Place remained her home.

Following the Queen's death the Mansion was bought by the Territory of Hawaii to serve as the official residence of its governors. In 1953, under the guidance of Hawaii's first governor of Hawaiian blood, Samuel Wilder King, the mansion was restored to the classic elegance of the monarchial period, in keeping with its history. Many of the original furnishings were returned by private owners.

Today, Queen Liliuokalani's grand piano, a gift from her people, stands in the reception hall. From this hall one may see, in the dining room between two windows, a majestic, full-length oil portrait of the Queen. Near by is her unused bedroom with its huge Victorian bed, feather kahilis and other original furnishings unchanged.

[67]

Iolani Palace as it appeared when finished in 1883. *Hawaiian Archives.*

Iolani Palace

THE FIRST Iolani Palace was built in 1845 upon land formerly occupied by a *heiau* (sacred temple). Of coral stone cut from the reef offshore, it was the residence of rulers Kamehameha III, IV and V and of King Lunalilo. The present palace, on the same site, was built by King Kalakaua, the cornerstone laid in December 1879 with Masonic Rites, as the king was a 33rd-degree Mason in Scottish Rite and Knight Templar of York.

Designer of the stately, ornate building was Australian architect T. J. Baker, who called it "American Florentine." On the south side of a spacious entrance hall with graceful staircase, the throne room was regal with red velvet carpet, gleaming crystal chandeliers, mirror-paneled walls and two French gilt throne chairs flanked by tall feather *kahilis*. Before the throne stood a gold-tipped *tabu* stick, emblem of royalty.

Opposite was the banquet hall, connected by folding doors with the smaller Blue Room, where comfortable armchairs, lounges, a piano and draperies in soft blue tones provided an informal background for after-dinner conversation.

On the second floor, facing the mountains, were Their Majesties' suites: the King's bedroom, library, dressing room and bath decorated in rich blue, the furniture ebony and gold; the Queen's suite, in rose, featured ceiling-high mirrors. Between the royal suites was a small breakfast and living room with easy chairs, book shelves and a grand piano. Two guest rooms, facing the sea, had French windows opening upon a broad *lanai*. In the basement were servants' quarters, kitchen, pantry and billiard room.

The elegance and beauty of the palace furnishings reflected King Kalakaua's own good taste for he had selected most of the things in Paris and had supervised every detail of arrangement, incorporating the many gifts received on his trip around the world.

Four ornamental iron gates to the Palace grounds each had a name and special purpose Kauike-aouli (named for Kamehameha III) was for state occasions only; Kinau gate was for official business; Hakaleleponi, for household troops and retainers; Likelike, a private entrance for members of the royal family. According to legend the Kauike-aouli gate, carefully locked at night, frequently swung open to allow entrance of a ghostly procession led by the beloved "Little King" himself.

On February 12, 1883, King Kalakaua and Queen Kapiolani were formally crowned in an octagonal pavilion erected for that purpose in front of the Palace, with which it was connected by a causeway. Later moved to a corner of the palace grounds, it now serves as bandstand.

Throne Room—These twin thrones at Honolulu's Iolani Palace are replicas of the original Hawaiian thrones (now in the Bishop Museum) used in monarchial days. Ida Naone, custodian of the Throne Room, standing by the thrones, wears a dress copied after one owned by Queen Liliuokalani. The feather *kahili* (standard) at left is the royal insignia used by Hawaiian rulers. *Hawaii Visitors Bureau.*

[71]

Mrs. Flora Hayes, authority on Hawaiiana, sometime movie actress, former legislator, costumed as a Lady at Court of King Kalakaua. *Courtesy Halekulani Hotel.* (Right) Aloha Festival. Annually in October, Hawaii stages a week or more of Hawaiian pageantry with an all-Hawaiian cast in the official events, including a King and Queen Consort costumed in the mode of ancient times. Here are "Their Majesties" (for 1961) King Sargeant Kahanamoku and his wife Anna as Queen Consort. "His Majesty" is a younger brother of far-famed Olympic swim champion Duke Kahanamoku. *Honolulu Advertiser.*

Provided with a proper setting for his lavish entertaining, King Kalakaua, known as "The Merrie Monarch of the Pacific" was host to artists, writers, musicians and scholars who came from all parts of the world to honor and enjoy this famous "Court of the Bohemians."

Iolani Palace now (1963) serves as the Executive Building for the State of Hawaii. When the projected Capitol Building is completed, world-famed Iolani Palace will be restored to its former regal glory.

Hanai-aka-malama

Hanai-aka-malama (Foster Child of Light), former home of Queen Emma, is a dignified frame house with pillared entrance set in the lush green of Nuuanu Valley. Built in 1843 as a country retreat for the royal family, its restoration was undertaken in 1914 by the Daughters of Hawaii, founded by descendants of American missionaries (membership now open to include native Hawaiians) "for the purpose of perpetuating the memory and spirit of old Hawaii."

Restoration and maintenance of this home of the greatly beloved Consort of Kamehameha IV has become a labor of love for the "Daughters," who continually seek royal relics with which to enhance the beauty and historic value of this gracious, intimate museum, their quest often rewarded by donations of privately owned treasures from monarchial days. The result is an enchanting restoration of an era long past.

At right of the entrance hall is Queen Emma's bedroom where, beside her large four-poster bed, stands the crib of her only child, the Little Prince of Hawaii. Glassed cabinets contain her wedding dress (made in New York), Brussels lace veil, slippers, and other costumes, including a beautiful black net dress worn at luncheon with Queen Victoria in Windsor Castle.

There are the Windsor uniforms of her husband, King Kamehameha IV; the made-in-Ireland lace christening robe of the Little Prince; his bright red "fireman's" suit; his personal silver; a porcelain bathtub from China; and, most valuable of all, a magnificent silver baptismal font sent for his christening by his godmother, Britain's Queen Victoria.

Queen Emma's jewelry cabinet contains an agate bracelet from Queen Victoria, enclosing her own portrait and lock of hair, a tiger-claw bracelet from an Indian Maharajah; an amethyst bracelet from the Duke of Edinburgh, and many other objects of beauty and value.

The "parlor" is rich with fine old furniture from England, Hawaiian feather kahilis, books (some autographed by famed authors of that day), portraits of Queen Emma's family and of European royalty presented to her during her trip abroad; among the latter are those of Queen Victoria, Prince Albert, Napoleon III and Empress Eugenie.

The most elegant room in the house is named for the Duke of Edinburgh, youngest son of Queen Victoria, who visited Hawaii in 1869. This room was added for a special party honoring him. Today, rich red velvet carpeting and crystal chandeliers provide appropriate setting for its handsome furnishings, which include Queen Emma's piano, treasure-filled cabinets and beautiful rosewood furniture from England. The walls form a gallery of royal portraits drawn by artists who sailed with early exploration ships from England and Europe.

Hanai-aka-malama, the Queen Emma Home Museum. *Hawaii Visitors Bureau.*

Built more than a century ago of coral blocks from the near-by reef and lumber from New England in clipper ships around Cape Horn, Kawaiahao is known as "The Westminster Abbey of Hawaii." *Hawaii Visitors Bureau.*

Kawaiahao Church

AN HISTORIC BUILDING closely associated with the lives of Hawaiians is Kawaiahao Church, the first church built by American missionaries who arrived in the Islands in 1820. The scene of royal marriages, funerals and christenings, it won the title of Hawaii's Westminster Abbey.

After Hawaii became a constitutional monarchy its rulers took the oath of office in Kawaiahao's hallowed halls; the first legislative sessions were held there, and it was there, in 1843, that King Kamehameha III proclaimed the historic words which became official motto for the Hawaiian Kingdom and is continued today as motto for the State of Hawaii: *Ua mau ke ea o ka aina i ka pono.* (The life of the land is perpetuated in righteousness).

The present structure, built in 1841, is the center of Hawaiian Congregationalists. Sunday services, conducted in both Hawaiian and English, attract many tourists who find there the soul of old Hawaii demonstrated in rich choral singing to touch the heart and sermons to stir the mind.

[77]

The Rev. Abraham K. Akaka, pastor of Kawaiahao Church, beloved of his own people and universally admired and respected. *Kawaiahao Church Archives.*

Pastor of Kawaiahao Church (1963) is the Reverend Abraham Akaka, a scholarly, deeply spiritual man who, in the words of *Star-Bulletin* editor William Ewing, has made of his church "a citadel of those virtues which Hawaiians brought to western civilization."

Born in 1917, Reverend Akaka has degrees in sociology and music, also that of Bachelor of Divinity from Chicago Theological Seminary of Chicago University. A frequent and popular speaker at church conventions on the mainland, he inspires gatherings with his spirituality and enchants them with his singing of Christian hymns in Hawaiian, to his own accompaniment on the ukulele. Wrote author Norman Lobsenz: "His every word and action are touched with grace. . . . He radiates a sense of peaceful calm."

Those American missionaries who built the first grass-thatched Kawaiahao Church upon ground hallowed in Hawaiian tradition may rest in peace. The seed they planted is thriving in the big coral church of today.

La Pietra

AMONG THE historic houses of Hawaii should be included one of modern structure which has been the center of much important entertaining since it was built in 1923. This is La Pietra, home of Mr. and Mrs. Walter Dillingham, a handsome Italian villa set upon the western talus of Diamond Head, surrounded by lush gardens and commanding a majestic view of mountains and sea.

La Pietra. Diamond Head home of Mr. and Mrs. Walter F. Dillingham. *Ralph Crane © Life Magazine.*

In its gracious drawing room, hung with priceless Flemish tapestries and opening upon a spacious Mediterranean courtyard, have been welcomed the great and near-great from all parts of the world, often at the request of official Washington, trusting to the Dillinghams the entertainment of important personages crossing the Pacific.

La Pietra, like many great mansions of the Old World, unsuited to the stream-lined living of today, should be preserved as a museum to commemorate that era when life was gracious and leisurely. This would be in keeping with its historic role as an extension of official Washington to its furthest outpost in the Pacific.

Diamond Head

DIAMOND HEAD, Hawaii's famed promontory, is widely known and loved. Its majestic, rugged profile has been painted by great artists, snapshot by tourists, filmed in movies, pictured on calendars and even on satin pillowtops for sale on River Street.

Its present name was bestowed by foreigners because at certain times of the day its cliff facing the sea glitters with mica flakes. But to ancient Hawaiians, a seafaring people, it was called Lae Ahi (Fire Headland) for the wood-fire kept burning on its crest at night as guide for sea traffic to the port of Honolulu.

Regarding it as a sacred mountain, the Hawaiians built important shrines upon its slopes, most sacred of which was Papa-enaena (Supreme Judgment Seat), dedicated to Ku, God of Power. It was there that Kamehameha the Great held formal ceremony commemorating the victory at Nuuanu Pali (1790) which gave him mastery of all the islands, when (as told in my book *The Lonely Warrior*):

Diamond Head and Waikiki Beach in the time of the Kamehamehas

by contemporary artist G. H. Burgess. *Honolulu Academy of Arts.*

"The heart of the defeated King Kalani-kupule was placed upon the sacrificial altar . . . as homage was paid by the forces of Kamehameha to the god Kukailimoku in gratitude for the great victory."

Another, smaller temple, Maka-huna, at the foot of Diamond Head *pali* (cliff) was dedicated to Kanaloa, God of the Seas and Sustainer of Life. This was religiously attended by fishermen and seamen. Also it was from this temple that announcement was made ending the annual Makahiki (Harvest Festival) as great *pahu* drums, resounding from the majestic cliff, carried the message across surf to sea where a ceremonial canoe bore the image of Lono, God of the Makahiki, to his home beyond the world.

On the peak of Diamond Head where the *Ahi* (fire) was tended there was a shrine to the God of the Winds to whom prayers and offerings were made for protection against the deadly Lehua—violent, sudden updrafts. The beacon fire meant guidance and protection of life to many a seaman. Thus Diamond Head, a monument to peace and beauty, is also of great historical significance, representing as it does the spirit of Lae Ahi, which served for thousands of years as a guiding light for humanity.

Papakolea

On July 9, 1921, the United States Congress, at the request of Hawaii's Delegate to Congress Prince Kalanianaole, passed a Hawaiian Homestead Act designed to place back upon the land of their ancestors natives of "not less than one half part Hawaiian blood." Later, when the constitutionality of the Act was tested, Judge H. E. Stafford ruled:

"This Act is unquestionably constitutional for the reason that a so-called civilized nation has a moral obligation to see that an aboriginal race over whose people and habitat they acquired jurisdiction and contract, be not exterminated."

Today homestead areas have been opened on several of the islands, each homesteader given a ninety-nine-year lease at a rental of one dollar per year. The land itself, still held by the Federal Government, will eventually pass to the State of Hawaii, but with certain controls retained by Congress.

Best known of the Homestead areas is Papakolea, at

the foot of Mt. Tantalus back of Honolulu, where more than 2000 Hawaiians live happily on former "Crown Lands" of the Hawaiian Kingdom. When the area was placed under the Hawaiian Homes Commission, some of those living there as squatters were descendants of original settlers who had followed the edict of King Kalakaua to his people that "Land belonging to the Crown is yours. Go and live upon it."

There for more than fifty years Hawaiians had lived on the side of the great mountain they love—without worldly goods but happy, proud, independent and "free like God wants us to live." Then, as now, freedom and happi-

A Papakolea home. *Honolulu Advertiser.*

The Author reading to Papakolea children. (Right) Papakolea family group. *Honolulu Advertiser.*

ness are values of first importance to Hawaiians, who for the most part remain uncontaminated by the greed and tensions of the city below them.

Each year the birthday of Prince Kalanianaole is celebrated with sports, musical programs and a great *luau*, followed by a visit to the Royal Mausoleum bearing flowers for his tomb. In a heartwarming ceremony prayers of gratitude for his protective care are made; then songs that he loved best are sung tenderly in his memory.

Ulu Mau Village is a bit of ancient Hawaiian community life set in a coconut grove in Ala Moana Beach Park only five minutes from the heart of Waikiki. Here can be seen the arts and crafts of old Hawaii demonstrated daily by Hawaiians skilled in their native culture. *Hawaii Visitors Bureau.*

A Polynesian Village

A POLYNESIAN VILLAGE, authentic in every detail and designed to preserve native Polynesian culture, is being built at Laie, thirty-eight miles from Honolulu on windward Oahu, upon twenty acres of land near the famed Mormon Temple (which attracts 150,000 visitors annually) and Church College. All three are projects of the Mormon Church, which, wrote Robert Louis Stevenson, "finds its way into the hearts of proud Polynesians as does no other Church."

In 1865 the Church bought 6000 acres at Laie, a beautiful seaside valley, and there established a community where native Hawaiians might preserve their own culture under church guidance. Hawaiians say, "They told the old folks to dedicate each piece of work to God as in the days of Kamehameha, and to laugh and sing while they worked," emphasizing, "They want us to work and to be good—but they want us to be happy too." This apparently is the secret of Mormon success in all undertakings.

"The purpose of the Village," said a Church leader, "is the preservation of Polynesian culture in undiluted form." Among those represented will be Samoans, Tahitians, Tongans, Fijians, natives of the Cook Islands, Maoris of New Zealand and, of course, Hawaiians. Houses representing each of these groups will be built by the natives themselves under supervision of Mormon missionaries who have served in their islands. A genuine Maori carved-house, brought from New Zealand, will be set up in its original form. "It is our desire to reproduce, not imitate, the culture of Polynesia," say the Mormon leaders.

As with other Mormon undertakings, all work is done by volunteers. "While the building itself is important," said one Churchman, "our biggest assignment always is the building of character. If we succeed in that we consider our job a success. If not, it is a failure." The seven-million-dollar Church College, completed in 1956, was built entirely by volunteers, from architect to day laborer.

With that special sense of beauty and good taste characteristic of all Mormon buildings, these three projects— Temple, College and Village—are set against a dramatic backdrop of mountains and each is enhanced with appropiate landscaping. The Temple is often compared to India's exquisite Taj Mahal.

When the Polynesian Village is completed, natives of each island represented will live permanently in the houses, the young people attending Church College, the old folks demonstrating their crafts for visitors. "Our aim," say Church leaders, "is to protect and faithfully preserve the culture of an artistic and generous people now fast vanishing."

For this, historians, scientists and peoples of all the world will owe the Mormons a debt of eternal gratitude.

[90]

The Mormon Temple at Laie faces the Church College across twenty acres upon which is being constructed a Polynesian Village where natives from all Polynesia will live and produce the arts and crafts and stage entertainment typical of their respective islands. *Church College.*

Coco Palms Hotel where ancient Hawaiian glamour and modern
luxury go hand in hand. *Senda*.

Two Hotels on Historic Sites

ON THE DRAMATICALLY beautiful island of Kauai, regal with majestic mountains and clothed in legendary lore, are two hotels designed to commemorate Hawaii's royal dynasties: Kamehameha the Great by Coco Palms and Kalakaua by Hanalei Plantation.

Coco Palms is built upon the former homesite of Queen Kapule, Consort of King Kaumualii, who ceded his island kingdom to Kamehameha the Great in 1810 to prevent its destruction by conquest. There in a setting of rare beauty has been created a Hawaiian atmosphere so authentic as to charm each visitor with the subtle fragrance of its historic past.

Bordering the *mauka* (inland) side of a lazy lagoon are grass-thatched cottages backed by a large coconut grove. On the opposite shore of the lagoon the dining room of the main building is open to the musical lap-lap of its waters. Larger and more conventional (but still atmospheric) buildings dot the grounds, surrounded by trees and flowering shrubs. The whole complex begets a feeling of romantic intimacy.

Each night at Coco Palms ancient rituals are enacted to the accompaniment of conch-shell trumpet and drums as *malo*-clad youths, carrying flaming torches, run along the banks of the lagoon and on out through the coconut grove, swinging their torches and lighting a constellation of other ones as they go. The setting, buildings, entertainment and devotion of those who serve in all capacities from management to yardboy revive the gentle voice of Old Hawaii.

Hanalei Plantation Hotel, set in a secluded eighteen-acre estate high above the excitingly beautiful Hanalei Valley, was the setting of "Plantation House" in the movie "South Pacific" and John DeCuir, designer of its sets, also designed the hotel which now tops a small knoll commanding a breathtakingly beautiful panorama of sea and mountains. Luxury guest-houses, each angled for a full view of the magnificent scenery, trail down the hillside to a white-sand beach.

In the entrance of the main building is "the torch that burns at noonday," insignia of the Kalakaua Dynasty. Gleaming crystal chandeliers, French-gilt chairs, striking draperies and handsome oil paintings create an elegance remindful of the splendorous reign of Hawaii's "Merrie Monarch." Nightly musical entertainment is of the same era, many of the songs having been written by the king himself.

Hanalei Plantation, like Coco Palms, is representative of the mood of this legendary island, called by Hawaiians "Kauai Hemolele" (Holy Land of Plenty). "Evil can never overcome Kauai," they say, "because of its powerful *mana* (spiritual quality)." The year 1960 saw a demonstration of this magic power.

[94]

Hanalei Plantation Hotel's view of clean, wide Hanalei Beach and evergreen rugged mountains. *Wenkam.*

A volcanic eruption on the island of Hawaii unleashed masses of acid-tainted clouds which swept northward, polluting each island in their path but, reported a news story, "As it neared Kauai a strange thing happened. The cloud folded back upon itself, turned, and moved away leaving the island uncontaminated."

Not strange, say the old Hawaiians.

Only beach and landing place on rugged Niihau, "Isle of Mystery," where Hawaiians live happily under the benign paternalism of the Robinson clan. *Hawaiian Archives.*

Niihau, "Isle of Mystery"

NIIHAU, seventeen miles off the coast of Kauai, is eighteen miles long, seven miles wide and has a 2000-foot mountain. Known as "The Isle of Mystery," it has become the nidus of fanciful lore full worthy of its dramatic history.

In 1863 it was bought for $10,000 from the Hawaiian Kingdom by the Sinclairs of Scotland who, under the leadership of Captain Francis Sinclair, moved to New Zealand in 1840 (where the Captain died) and, twenty-three years later, to Hawaii. The family at that time consisted of Mrs. Sinclair, sixty-three; daughter Jean, with her sea-captain husband Thomas Gay and their five children; daughter Helen and son Aubrey Robinson; and three unmarried Sinclair children, James, Frank and young daughter Anne.

They arrived in Hawaii aboard their own barque, *Bessie*, which carried also sheep, cattle, a milch cow, a large library of fine books, a piano, quantities of Victorian furniture and ample food for all hands, man and beast.

Living on Niihau at the time of its purchase were about 300 Hawaiians who quickly became contented members of the Sinclair menage and the special charge of Mrs. Sinclair, who set up a paternalistic pattern for their care and protection which has been continued by her descendants.

After establishing a great baronial estate on the island's seventy-two square miles, the Sinclairs bought several acres on Kauai where they built another large house, thereafter dividing their time between the two homes, commuting by whale-boat and communicating by carrier pigeon.

Under the always undisputed control of the intelligent, courageous and strong-willed Mrs. Sinclair, who wore feminine ruffled bonnets and lacy neck-pieces but ruled her family with matriarchial efficiency, the Clan Sinclair increased in number and prosperity. Daughter Anne married an adventurous Norwegian of distinguished lineage, Valdemar Knudsen, and their children were to establish two prominent island families: the Knudsens and von Holts. In 1885 grandson Aubrey married his cousin Alice Gay (who had inherited grandmother Sinclair's matriarchial abilities) and they had five children. The roots of the Clan were becoming deeply, securely established in Hawaiian soil.

The Sinclairs had chosen Hawaii as their home largely because of their liking for the Hawaiian rulers, especially King Kamehameha IV and his gracious part-British Consort Queen Emma. After overthrow of the Hawaiian Monarchy the Robinson branch of the family, reserved by nature, withdrew from the local scene and to this day continues to live aloof from other residents of Kauai. Members of the younger generation are educated at American universities and usually marry "mainlanders."

They are described as "righteous, conscientious citizens," emulating always the Mother of the Clan, of whom a visitor wrote: "Her integrity and strength of character impresses everyone."

"Mother" Sinclair died in 1892 when she was ninety-two. Not long before her death a writer described her as "beautiful in her old age, light in figure and step as a young girl . . . conversant in theology and politics, devoted to her children but still firmly holding the reigns of management." Almost to the day of her death she took a brisk ride on her favorite horse, wearing always her feminine ruffled bonnets and lacy neck-pieces.

Today, after purchase of other family interests, Niihau and the land holdings on Kauai are owned by descendants of Aubrey Robinson, whose son Alymer (born 1888) makes the little island his particular project, ruling it with a firm, paternalistic hand, protecting and nurturing the 300 Hawaiians who live there and excluding all visitors. This latter ruling arouses the ire of professional "do-gooders" and wily politicians who rant about "needed reforms" and "opening up the island to democracy." Periodically these groups attempt to destroy this one last place in Hawaii where there are peace, serenity, no automobiles, telephones, movies, TV, liquor, jails (because there is no crime), juvenile delinquency and—no ulcers.

Chief industry of the island is ranching, which supports 1700 cattle and about 5000 merino sheep. The cowboys ride blooded Arabian horses and after work hunt wild pigs in the mountains, fish in the sea or "just sit round and play the ukulele." There is free housing for all, each house surrounded by a large vegetable garden cared for by the wives. Sugar, rice, flour and other needs are bought wholesale by Mr. Robinson for the people.

An island school carries through the sixth grade and

any boy or girl who wishes higher education is placed in the desired school by Mr. Robinson, who pays the bills. Monthly physical examinations are made by a Kauai physician who pronounces the people "grand physical specimens of the human race."

There is one church, attended by everyone on Sundays, and as evidence of the island's rich spiritual quality inhabitants report that sharks swimming in waters surrounding the island "never bite anybody because their hearts, like ours, are filled with *aloha*."

On Saturday nights there is a community party with music, dancing and bountiful refreshments. The people say, "We have everything worth while here. We are happier than the people in Honolulu." Of this Eden existing quietly, happily in the noise-maddened world of today, the *Boston Herald* once asked editorially:

"Pan American, when does the next plane leave for Niihau?"

Only once has the serenity of the little island been broken. On December 7, 1941, the Japanese pilot of a plane damaged in the attack on Pearl Harbor landed on Niihau. He was joined immediately by two local Japanese working on the island and the three set about to terrorize the native Hawaiians, who, after hastily rushing their wives and children to the mountains, set signal fires for Mr. Robinson on Kauai. However, he was unable to send help at once because of military restrictions.

For one week the three Japanese continued to harass the Hawaiians but finally, in the words of Benjamin Kanehele, "They went too far." Whereupon the powerfully built Hawaiian picked up the squat little Japanese pilot by neck and leg as he would a sheep and bashed him against a stone wall. That ended the trouble with him. The

Island-born Japanese immediately committed suicide and the alien fled to the mountains.

Later, in reporting the episode to army officials, Kanehele said calmly, "He shot me once. He shot me twice. Then he shot me the third time and that made me mad!"

When details of the affair reached Honolulu people wondered, fearfully, what might happen should the enemy return. The comment going around was "Don't ever shoot a Hawaiian the *third* time!"

This, then, is a brief outline of the story of Hawaii's "Isle of Mystery" where the pattern of seclusion and protection set up by the wise, humanitarian Mrs. Sinclair is continued today by Harvard-graduate grandson Alymer, "who speaks Hawaiian like flowing music" and keeps tight, paternalistic guard over his "right little island" in the manner of the baronial estates of 17th-century Scotland, his modern-day fief the only place in all Hawaii where native Hawaiians retain their ancestral cultural pattern and their racial integrity.

The Saga of the Sinclairs is worthy of a great epic poem based upon the redoubtable Mother of the Clan, Mrs. Francis Sinclair, in whose honor New Zealand named a towering mountain peak Mount Sinclair.

And This from a Native of Niihau

Mrs. Jean Keale of Niihau, mother of three children, educated at Kamehameha Schools (all costs paid by Mr. Robinson, owner of Niihau), made these comments while teaching Hawaiian at the University of Hawaii Summer School in 1963:

"I prefer life on Niihau to that of Honolulu. We are happier than the people here. You have too much of every-

Mrs. Jean Keale, a native of Niihau, says "We are closer to God." *University of Hawaii.*

thing: too many people, too much money, life is too complex. You say we are poor. By whose standards are we being judged? Our men are well paid on the ranch but we just put it away on pay day and it is still there the next month. We never think about money, never have to carry it around to pay for things.

"We go hunting and fishing for food and are allowed to clear as much land as we want for planting vegetables. Mr. Robinson provides us with canned goods and basic foods. He is like a father to us, does everything for our good.

"Here in Honolulu people compete with and often dislike each other. On Niihau there is no need to compete so we have *aloha* in our hearts for each other. We are a church-going people. We like to sing hymns and to pray. I think we are closer to God than the people of Honolulu."

The Fabulous Parker Ranch

In the year 1809 John Palmer Parker of Newton, Massachusetts, age nineteen, shipped aboard a windjammer to see the world. After five years at sea he settled in Hawaii, where Kamehameha the Great, liking the young man, gave him vast acreage on the island of Hawaii and the hand in marriage of his granddaughter High Chiefess Kipikane.

Today (1962) the almost 300,000-acre Parker Ranch, running 37,000 head of Hereford cattle and 5000 sheep, with 1500 fine horses, is owned by sixth-generation descendant Richard Kaleioku Smart, a tall, handsome multimillionaire who, until 1959, followed a theatrical career in Europe and America while able managers maintained the famed Parker Ranch in the grand manner of his ancestors. Now, to the joy of Hawaiians, Richard is "home to stay."

The Parker family has produced many picturesque personalities, one of the most noted being Richard's great-grandfather, the fabulous Samuel Kealiilani Parker, who was known as "Kamuela, Lord of Mana" and was always described in superlatives: "The handsomest man at the Court of King Kalakaua . . . the greatest wit . . . most beloved by women, most extravagant . . ." Legends concerning him are legion and all glow with affectionate admiration. When "Kamuela" went forth, white-clad from top to toe, riding a white stallion, himself and steed lei-bedecked, it was a sight to stir all hearts. The entire countryside turned out to pay homage.

A member of the House of Lords and, later, Minister of Foreign Affairs in Queen Liliuokalani's Cabinet, "Kamuela" conducted a Court of his own at Mana rivaling that at Iolani Palace in Honolulu and with entertainment lavish, elegant, sumptuous, gay, joyous and continuous. He was the uncrowned King of the Island of Hawaii.

Parker legends center next around Kamuela's granddaughter, Thelma Parker Smart, who, following the death of her father John III, inherited the great ranch when she was less than a year old. Stories about her, warmed with fervent affection and tinged with sorrow, are as numerous and as enduring as those of Kamuela. "Sensitive, warm of heart and delicately beautiful," she was loved by people of all races. The ranch cowboys worshiped her and she, returning their love, established a trust providing that one-fourth of the ranch's yearly income be used for their benefit. It has never been changed.

In 1912 Thelma, then eighteen years old, married Henry Gaillard Smart of Virginia. Richard was born the following year. In the spring of 1914 Thelma and Henry went to Paris, where a daughter was born but lived only a few months. Learning that Thelma had developed tuberculosis, the young couple started back to their island home but death ended the journey for her in San Francisco.

News of the beloved Thelma's death brought forth a

Richard Kaleioku Smart, owner of Parker Ranch. *Parker Ranch.*
(Right) Thelma Parker Smart in wedding dress, 1912. *Courtesy Richard Smart.*

torrent of sorrow unequaled in island history. The Parker Ranch cowboys were "wild with passionate grief," Hawaiians wept and wailed and all others mourned her with sorrowful hearts. Even today many of the older Hawaiians cannot speak of her without shedding tears. One year later widower Henry Gaillard Smart died at his home in Virginia.

Richard was not yet two years old when these tragedies struck. For a second time the great Parker Ranch was passed on to a small child. Taken in charge immediately by his grandmother, Richard thereafter was to spend his life between the ranch and her home in California, where he received his education from private tutors, public schools and

Stanford University. Even as a child his great love for the theater was evident. He designed and directed marionette shows, sang his way through high school and won a state-wide Shakespeare contest. After graduating from Stanford, he joined the Pasadena Playhouse.

In 1936 Richard was married to socially prominent Patricia Haven-Monteagle of Burlingame. They had two sons, Anthony and Gaillard. Seven years later they were divorced and thereafter his life was devoted entirely to the theater. Following wartime USO concerts, his first important role was the lead in "Bloomer Girl," which ran for more than a year on Broadway.

In January, 1962, Richard and son "Tony" (who has prepared himself for ranching with an agricultural course at Vermont University and business training at Stanford) commemorated their "return home" and also the anniversary of the founding of the Parker Ranch with a week-end houseparty for a thousand guests, climaxed by a great ball in the manner of their famed ancestor, "Kamuela, Lord of Mana."

Richard now has an imaginative plan under way for restoration of all ranch buildings, public and private, in the style of Hawaii's monarchial era. First restored was the original coral-stone home of John Palmer Parker at Mana. This has been made a museum for family heirlooms, ranging from a crudely carved koa bed from John the First to dainty belongings of the lovely Thelma.

Next restored and greatly expanded was Puuopelu, the 100-year-old home of John the Second for use as Richard's own residence. There, spacious rooms are filled with elegant furnishings from Europe, blended harmoniously with ancient Hawaiian artifacts. Lights of gleaming chandeliers hanging from high ceilings reflect in long wall mirrors a dazzling display of highly polished calabashes as well as handsome modern furniture.

A large ancient "pig-board" (wooden platter) mellowed by the meat and memories of many a *luau,* glass-encased, serves as coffee table for a tufted banquette of rich velvet. The vivid colors of a velvet carpet splashed with clusters of deep pink roses are repeated in a flower garden bordering the living-room terrace. Throughout the house beautiful oil portraits of the lovely Thelma continue her influence upon the lives of her descendants.

Restoration of this little empire in the mood and appearance of Hawaii's glamorous monarchial past is extended also to the houses of ranch employees, which, painted in gay colors and adorned with rococo trim, make driving along country roads through rolling green pastures a sheer delight.

Recently Richard has had the ranch made a trust, the income of which (after allotments to Tony and Gil) is to be used for its enrichment and development, for the welfare of the employees and for charitable purposes. It was done to insure that this majestic and historic domain, stretching from the cold mountain slopes of Mauna Loa to the warm golden sands of the seashore, shall be perpetuated forever as the Parker Ranch.

Imaginative, ambitious founder John Palmer Parker, who loved Hawaii and Hawaiians with whole-hearted devotion, would be pleased.

Pele the Fire Goddess. Crayon by Madge Tennant 1943.

Pele, Goddess of Fire and Volcanoes

PELE, GODDESS OF FIRE, has dominated Hawaiian legendry for countless centuries and even today, in a burgeoning civilization which scoffs at all things not provable by mathematics, she continues her hold upon the hearts and imaginations of men. Stories concerning her are legion, undying, constantly in creation, believed in and abetted by many non-Hawaiians who have absorbed the mysticism of the land.

Pele's immortality might be explained by the belief that she is part deity, part human. According to legend, she was born on a mystic South Sea island, Kuai-he-lani, "which floated free in the ocean and was not rooted in one spot." Her father, reportedly, was Ku, God of Power; her mother, Haumea, his human wife. (Like those of ancient Greece, the Hawaiian gods often took mortals to wife.) Pele's ability to assume human form is therefore understandable.

Ancient chants describe the proud goddess as possessing supernatural beauty with "gleaming black hair, eyes that shone with fire, a back as straight as a cliff and breasts rounded like the moon." She was also exceedingly willful.

Despite orders that she was not to meddle with the fire-making activities of her elder brother Lono-maku, she did so one day and set a fire so spectacular and violent that it destroyed a large part of the island. The inhabitants, infuriated, drove her into the sea, which was set in roaring motion by the Sea Goddess, Namaka-o-kahai, Pele's elder sister, who had always been jealous of the beautiful and imperious Fire Goddess.

Immediately to her rescue came the god Ku. Secretly proud of his spirited daughter, he sent a magic canoe, *Honua-ia-kea*, manned by the paddlers Current, Tide and Whirlwind, to carry her northward in search of a new homeland. Joining her on the journey were her three admiring brothers, Ka-moko-alii, God of the Sharks, Kao-mea-lani, God of Vapor and Gentle Rains (later to form misty clouds over her volcanic pits) and Lono-makua, who carried a lighted torch to guide them. Also with them was their youngest sister, dainty little Hi'iaka, whom Pele "carried close to her heart."

Swept along by strong currents and protected by the special favor of the gods the magic canoe bearing Pele and her entourage was borne swiftly north to the Hawaiian Islands, where the first landing was made on the small island of Niihau. After a brief rest the party moved on to the near-by island of Kauai, which they found enchantingly beautiful. There, at Haena point, Pele saw a handsome young mortal, Lohiau, with whom she promptly fell in love. Taking the form of a beautiful young maiden, she sought him out and won his heart.

For many months Pele and Lohiau lived together in unalloyed bliss. Then the restless goddess, desiring an even

Temple of Lono, God of Agriculture and Sports, in the City of Refuge at Kealakekua, Kona, showing Captain Cook being received as Lono incarnate, returned as promised in ancient legends. He chanced to arrive at the time of the annual Makahiki, native Thanksgiving Festival of which Lono was patron. Ignorance of language and legend prevented Cook and staff knowing the ceremony was anything more than Hawaiian hospitality. *John Webber 1779*. (This temple and others in the area, including replicas of the idols, are now being restored by the U.S. National Park Service, to which the City of Refuge was recently turned over.)

more perfect home for her lover, set sail again in her sacred canoe, moving from island to island, lighting her fires as she went until she came at last to the island of Hawaii, where, sighting a great mountain, she cried happily, "This shall be my home. And I will call it Mauna Loa for the journey has been long."

Pele's love affair with the handsome Lohiau, oft repeated, forms one of the great love stories of Hawaiian legendry and, like many another historic love story, it ended in tragedy. While preparing an elaborate home in Mauna

Loa for her lover she sent her young sister Hi'iaka to guide him on the journey from Kauai. But the seas were turbulent and they were long in coming. On arrival, Pele, insane with jealousy, slew them both with an outburst of fiery lava.

And to this day, when she goes forth on a rampage of destruction it is believed she does so out of remorse for that rash act.

After sovereignty of the Islands was transferred to the United States in 1900 Pele sulked in her volcanic pit for several years. Then she began to appear throughout the islands in many places, in many forms, reported by both *haoles* and natives. In anticipation of her return, Hawaiians gathered by the Halemaumau pit on the date prophesied by *kahunas* as the time of her reappearance in fiery form. A newsman who slipped into the crowd unnoticed wrote:

"Priests chanted the Pele *mele*, dancers performed ritualistic ceremonies, offerings of *ohelo* berries and *lehua* blossoms were dropped reverently into the pit. Then, suddenly, the moon burst through an embankment of dark clouds throwing an eerie light on an old woman standing on the edge of the pit. An aged priest chanted. The old woman lifted her hands in response—then vanished in a burst of flames which arose from the depths of the crater. Instantly the entire pit which moments before had been filled only with smoke and sulphurous fumes became a roaring inferno of seething lava with fountains thrown 300 feet into the air."

Pele takes many forms when appearing before human beings. She may come as an old woman begging food or as a beautiful young girl seeking love. A strict precept of ancient Hawaii was "Never injure a woman. It might be Pele!" Once a powerful chief on the island of Hawaii offered an insult to an old woman, who angrily stamped her foot, causing the earth to open and pour forth hot lava

Captain Cook's ships coming to anchor in Kealakekua Bay off the City of Refuge and Hawaiians thinking that Lono had at long last kept his promise someday to return in person. *John Webber 1779.*

which rolled in fiery fury down the hillside, destroying the chief's lands as it went. And atop the flow, long hair streaming in the breeze, rode a beautiful young woman recognized too late as the Goddess Pele.

Animals are aware of Pele's presence. When she is abroad in the land dogs howl piteously, horses rear and plunge, cats stand with arched backs. In modern times her power extends to mechanical things: cars stop suddenly and cannot be started again although nothing is mechanically wrong. Pele again, people say.

But she is not always destructive. Many Hawaiians report her assistance in times of stress. "Even when she seems to be cruel she is on our side," say the old folks. She is their secret weapon. By means entirely satisfactory to themselves, her actions, both good and bad, can be so interpreted. Such is the power of infinite faith.

Even today in the prosaic world of the 1960s, the goddess continues to warn of coming eruptions by various means: mysterious lights, inexplicable happenings, personal appearances, all of which are duly reported by the newspapers. Occasionally she appears as "Mauna Loa's Phantom Dog"—a small white dog seen wandering shortly before an eruption on barren lava mountain slopes where, according to staff members of the Volcanic Observatory who saw him prior to the 1959 and 1960 eruptions, "There is neither food nor water for miles around—yet he appears to be fat, sleek and well fed. It is very mysterious."

Not at all mysterious, say Hawaiians.

In December, 1935, a violent eruption of the volcano sent a wide stream of lava flowing slowly, relentlessly down the mountainside toward the town of Hilo. The residents, alarmed, begged for government assistance. A scientist suggested bombing the flow to divert its course. The army agreed to furnish the bombers.

Hawaiians warned: "Let her alone. Pele is just scaring some people who insulted her. She will stop soon." Unheeding, army planes dropped bombs on December 27. A few days later the flow stopped short of Hilo. The old folks muttered, "Watch out! You have angered Pele. She will have her revenge."

Less than a month later, on January 24, 1936, two bombers carrying eight men collided in midair over Luke Field on Oahu and fell crashing to earth. The planes were those used in the bombing of the lava flow. Six of the men aboard had done the bombing. They were all killed. The two who had not participated in the bombing bailed out safely. Wrote newsman George Wright:

"The old Hawaiians predicted disaster . . . now they are whispering. . . . Tragedy seems to follow the trail of the dead men's ashes carried to the mainland on the US transport *Republic*. When the ship arrived at its destination Captain McClellan, the skipper, was missing. That mystery has not been solved. Did the curse of Pele follow this

Monument at Kealakekua commemorating Captain Cook's landing and death when, having sailed at close of the Makahiki, in accordance with the legend, he was forced to return to repair a storm-damaged mast. When his divinity was doubted, a dagger test proved him mortal. *Hawaiian Archives.*

vessel even as the curse of ancient Egyptian kings is said to follow those who violate their tombs?

"Coincidence, of course. Pele is a myth from ancient times. A volcano is merely a natural phenomenon which primitive minds personify as a goddess. Science laughs at Pele and drops bombs on her home. When men who did it meet with strange accidents it is just coincidence. When the Captain of the ship which carries their ashes vanishes in the night, it is another coincidence. . . .

"But Hawaiians do not talk of coincidences. They do not wonder about it at all."

An anonymous poet contributed this thought:

They are not dead they are but sleeping
The gods of old Hawaii.
I have heard them in the still of night
Whisperings of huge portent in the seething surf;
They are more than winds in palm trees
More than surging seas.

I have heard the undertones of power;
Of fierceness and of strength;
I have heard the minor tones of nostalgia
Of sadness and dreams.
No, they are not dead, they are but sleeping
The gods of old Hawaii.

INDEX